BRIGHT SHENG

NORTHERN LIGHTS

FOR VIOLONCELLO AND PIANO

(SCORE)

ED 4718
First Printing: October 2018

ISBN: 978-1-5400-2751-1

G. SCHIRMER, Inc.

DISTRIBUTED BY

 HAL•LEONARD®

7777 W. BLUEMOUND RD. P.O. BOX 13819 MILWAUKEE, WI 53213
www.halleonard.com
www.musicsalesclassical.com

Composer's Note

Folk music has been my fascination and creative resource for over four decades. In the early 1970's, I first became infatuated with the folks songs of Qinghai (eastern Tibet), a rare fusion and crossover of several ethnic folk cultures in the region. Subsequently, during my undergraduate years at The Shanghai Conservatory of Music, I further systematically studied Chinese folk music traditions. Shortly after I moved to the United States in the early 1980's, my interest was broadened to include music cultures surrounding China, and the relationship of how these cultures had influenced, intermingled, and infiltrated each other. This led to my series of studies of the music cultures along the Silk Road, an ancient trading route between the old empires of China and Rome, while helping my friend Yo-Yo Ma launch the Silk Road Project. I have also been captivated by American folk music for decades, especially bluegrass and country music; and it has long been my hope to find pretext to include these elements in my work.

My friends Inger and Bill Ginsberg live in New York City and in Hellen, Norway, where Inger was born. During one conversation, Bill, well-versed in the Norwegian culture, introduced me to Norwegian and Scandinavian folk music. I became even more excited when, after further examination, I noticed its kinship with some forms of American country music, such as Appalachian and bluegrass.

In many ways, composing music in various styles is similar to a writer using different languages; and the work is usually most effective when the author is most comfortable with the language. On the other hand, for a range of reasons, many literary giants attempted their second (or even third) language to great results. *Northern Lights* is my first attempt to integrate Norwegian/Scandinavian folk music; and it probably has a linguistic accent. However, as a student who is embarking his first performance with a newly-learned language, I am fully excited with the probability of including another tongue in my works.

The title of the work, *Northern Lights*, refers to an astronomical natural phenomenon also known as polar lights (aurora polaris), which are shafts or curtains of fantastically colored light visible on occasion in the night sky, particularly in countries of the polar regions, such as Norway.

—Bright Sheng

NORTHERN LIGHTS *was commissioned by*
The Chamber Music Society of Lincoln Center, La Jolla Music Society,
and Bergen Festival by a generous gift from William Ginsberg in honor of his wife, Inger G. Ginsberg.

The premieres of this work were performed by:
Audun Sandvik, violoncello, and Kristian Lindberg, piano
World premiere: July 3, 2010, Troldhauge [Grieg's house], Norway

Lynn Harrell, violoncello, and Victor Asuncion, piano
US premiere: August 8, 2010, La Jolla SummerFest

Alisa Weilerstein, violoncello, and Inon Barnatan, piano
New York City premiere: November 9, 2010, Alice Tully Hall, Lincoln Center for the Performing Arts

The work has been recorded and is available on NAXOS 8.579014
Julian Schwarz, violoncello, and Marika Bournaki, piano

duration circa 25 minutes

Information on Bright Sheng and his works is available at www.musicsalesclassical.com

to Inger G. Ginsberg

NORTHERN LIGHTS

Bright Sheng

I

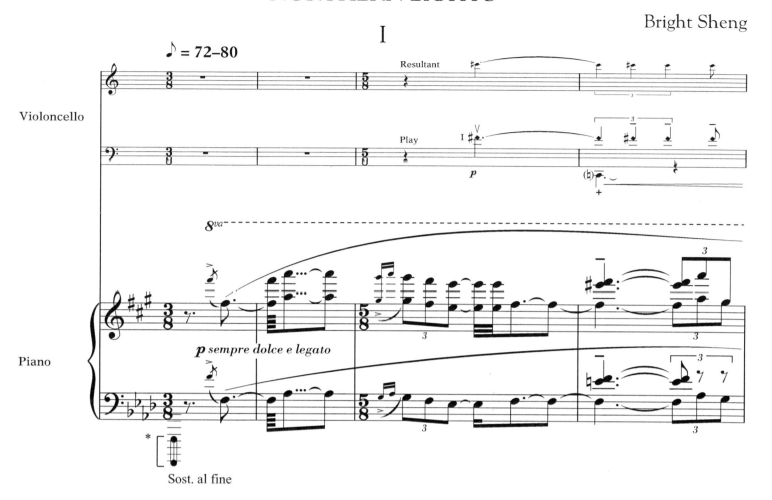

Violoncello

Piano

* Sost. al fine

*Silently depress all keys (black and white) and hold with sostenuto pedal until end of movement.

Più mosso ♪ = 80–88